1595

D1376354

Baby
Eagles

Mary Elizabeth Salzmann

Consulting Editor, Diane Craig, M.A./Reading Specialist

Sandcastle

An Imprint of Abdo Publishing
www.abdopublishing.com

www.abdopublishing.com

Published by Abdo Publishing, a division of ABDO, PO Box 398166, Minneapolis, Minnesota 55439. Copyright © 2015 by Abdo Consulting Group, Inc. International copyrights reserved in all countries. No part of this book may be reproduced in any form without written permission from the publisher. SandCastle™ is a trademark and logo of Abdo Publishing.

Printed in the United States of America, North Mankato, Minnesota

102014
012015

Editor: Alex Kuskowski
Content Developer: Nancy Tuminelly
Cover and Interior Design and Production: Mighty Media, Inc.
Photo Credits: Shutterstock, Thinkstock, Reese F. Lukei, Jr., Research Associate, The Center for Conservation Biology at the College of William & Mary

Library of Congress Cataloging-in-Publication Data

Salzmann, Mary Elizabeth, 1968- author.
 Baby eagles / Mary Elizabeth Salzmann.
     pages cm. -- (Baby animals)
 Audience: Ages 4-9.
 ISBN 978-1-62403-508-1
1. Eagles--Infancy--Juvenile literature. I. Title.
 QL696.F32S25 2015
 598.9'42139--dc23
                          2014023424

SandCastle™ Level: Beginning

SandCastle™ books are created by a team of professional educators, reading specialists, and content developers around five essential components—phonemic awareness, phonics, vocabulary, text comprehension, and fluency—to assist young readers as they develop reading skills and strategies and increase their general knowledge. All books are written, reviewed, and leveled for guided reading, early reading intervention, and Accelerated Reader® programs for use in shared, guided, and independent reading and writing activities to support a balanced approach to literacy instruction. The SandCastle™ series has four levels that correspond to early literacy development. The levels are provided to help teachers and parents select appropriate books for young readers.

EMERGING · **BEGINNING** · TRANSITIONAL · FLUENT

Contents

Baby Eagles

Baby eagles **hatch** out of eggs.

Baby eagles are very **fluffy**. They are usually white or gray.

They grow up in nests.
Eagles' nests are high in
tall trees.

Mother eagles bring food to their babies. They eat mostly fish.

The mother eagle chews up the food. Then she feeds it to her babies.

Mother eagles guard their nests.

Baby eagles stay in their nests for 8 to 14 weeks.

Baby eagles turn brown as they get older.

They learn how to fly.
Then they can live on
their own.

Did You Know?

- ▶ Bald eagles' heads turn white when they are three to five years old.

- ▶ Baby eagles are called eaglets.

- ▶ Only bald eagles and golden eagles live in the United States.

- ▶ **Female** eagles are larger than **male** eagles.

Eagle Quiz

Read each sentence below. Then decide whether it is true or false.

1. Baby eagles **hatch** out of eggs.

2. Baby eagles are very **fluffy**.

3. Mother eagles don't bring food to their babies.

4. Mother eagles do not guard their nests.

5. Baby eagles turn black as they get older.

Answers: 1. True 2. True 3. False 4. False 5. False

Glossary

female – being of the sex that can produce eggs or give birth. Mothers are female.

fluffy – covered with soft hair or feathers.

hatch – to break out of an egg.

male – being of the sex that can father babies. Fathers are male.